HOW WE ARE NOT ALONE

new and selected poems

by Maya Stein

How We Are Not Alone: New and selected poems
All writing and photographs © 2012 by Maya Stein

All rights reserved. No portion of this publication may be reproduced or reprinted without express written permission from the author. For more information, email mayarachelstein@gmail.com

table of contents

introduction 14

without fail 17
first love 19
everything new again 20
the view from 20D 21
a dime in the asphalt 23
phantom love 25
tangerines 28
breakfast: meditations on love 29
orange towels 32
dressing up for the doctor 33
free-throw 36
how to start over 38
clover 40
flight 41
instantaneous 43
substitutes 44
life lessons from the street musicians 46
suddenly, an orchard 47
a short letter to an old love 48
strand 50
luck and other variables 52
with the wineglass almost empty 53
how to get everything you've ever wanted 54
dayenu 56
believe 58
something for everyone 59

strong	61
empty	63
what brings you to the next morning	65
the luxury of failure	67
poem after surgery	69
let it be now	71
the beauty of grief	73
the velocity of tulips	75
sitting Shiva for Muriel Katz	77
intermission	80
exit	82
placeholder	84
the recital	86
how we are not alone	88
begin here	90
what happiness was	93
to love what we love	94
yes	96
the window seat	99
toward summit	100
witness	102
unpublished work	104

to light and to shadow,

to magic, to error,

to solitude, to company,

to fire and to earth,

to love and to uncertainty

to risk and to hope,

and all of the muses in between…

introduction

It is hard to know how to introduce this particular collection of writing. I suspect the reason for this is that it formed so incrementally, without a particular form or trajectory in my mind. All of the poems included here originally appeared and are still housed on my blog, "One Paragraph at a Time" (www.papayamaya.blogspot.com). In some cases, I have returned to them and tinkered. In others, I've left them intact. And though I've considered the thread and rhythm and theme of the book (and culled the writing that fit most comfortably within that structure) I haven't spent months thinking about the poems' order of appearance (save for when I wrote them chronologically), or worked with an editor to do any fine-tuning. I haven't given the manuscript to an intimate group of readers for feedback. I realize I could have done all of these, but it felt more important to simply get it out there, plain and simple.

In a way, I wanted to preserve the blog's mission statement, which doubles as its subhead: "This is not about getting it right, figuring things out, or hitting a bull's-eye. This is not about an obsession with word choice or an exacting eye on grammatical correctness. This is not about pulling out all the stops with tricky literary devices. This is about looking at life one paragraph at time." And while the poems herein are hardly paragraphs (though some are), there is a definite looseness around "the rules" – inconsistent capitalization, punctuation, and the like.

As a child, I was often in a state of musing exploration, uncovering bits of things on my excursions outside, hunkering down and peering at the ephemera of nature from an intimate closeness. I was less concerned about the big picture, where everything fit and why, but instead was content to sift and gather and look at the insides. I loved taking apart electronics, holding all those tiny screws and bolts in my hands, then attempting the task of reassembly…though sometimes I didn't get everything back to its right place. It didn't matter. I was passionate about the microscopic aspect of the thing, its elements, its building blocks. It was less important to me how it came together.

I had a similar affection and attitude toward language. I was adept at rhyming and spelling, very facile with the sound and feel of words, but I was less successful at piecing them into coherent thoughts. I was told frequently by teachers and my parents to "get to the main idea" in the papers I wrote for school, or the stories I told out loud. What I remember is struggling to have the arc close, for the beginning to get to the end. I had to learn these mechanics, had to struggle through many rounds of drafts, but eventually I figured out how to write successful academic papers, and this sailed me through the rest of high school and college without a lot of fanfare. Still, at the heart of it, I was drawn intuitively to a more creative navigation of language, and I see that this instinct to wander and explore and muse and take apart was probably the most powerful tool and resource in developing a relationship to poetry that has kept me writing since.

It's funny, but I often feel as if I am writing the same poem over an over again, in a wonderfully impossible attempt to "get it right." There's something about that pursuit, that dig, that uncovering of language, which keeps revealing to me different ways of telling the story. So writing has been a place for me to get messy and try things out, find new angles and perspectives, and most – and most significantly – to play. Even when the poems are addressing a difficult subject, what drives the writing is always a sense of deep wonder and learning, and I know that what keeps me putting pen to paper, or uploading new posts to the blog, is a desire to see life more clearly, and to share these explorations and (occasional) epiphanies with others. Having a public space to connect around these poems and the experiences they are responding to has gifted me an additional sense of understanding, compassion, and company. I can think of no better comfort when it comes to navigating the complexities and mysteries of living than to reach out and find others who "get it," who are traveling a similar journey.

This book is dedicated to the readers of my blog, and to those who have been following my work since I first began posting publicly in 2004. A special thank-you goes to Gail Henderson-Belsito, Patricia Ryan Madson, Dale Favier, Kate Johnson, Di Mackey, GoGo, Hashi, Jaime Brandel, Mom on the Alert, Margie, Wenda Nairn, Pamela Hunt, Jen Gray and Kirsten Lee Soares and other longstanding friends who have been particularly attentive to and supportive since the beginning. And to Christine Mason Miller, Jean Reinhold, Celeste Tibbets, and Amy Tingle Williamson for deepening the conversation. And to Deena Metzger, for the way her teachings have continued to sharpen my vision. Hearty hugs goes to Patti Digh and Andrea Scher, who have generously shared a goodly number of my writings on their blogs (www.37days.com and www.superherolife.com, respectively) over the years. Also, a deep bow of gratitude to Sherry Reichert Belul for the constancy of her energy for spreading the word. And a big, long squeeze to Laurie Wagner for sharing so many of these poems with her Wild Writing students and being a constant presence and source of inspiration to stay true to my path. And finally, a sheepish grin to Heloise Jones, for the not-so-gentle reminder to get this collection out the door at last.

Enjoy.

Maya Stein
September 2012

16

without fail

The avocado tree outside the sliding glass doors
of my living room sprang from a series of pits
two young girls tossed from their bedroom balcony
in various fits of boredom and scientific curiosity.
Or so my landlord tells me, his daughters now
grown and sprouting seeds of their own,
MBAs, New York careers, the lot of it.
He points out the other haphazard, accidental bloomings -
a cherry tree, orange, plum - but says, with a grimace
and an odd sense of satisfaction,
that none of the fruit is edible.
I try anyway.
Steal down the trap door to the garden
on a day he's not here, spend an hour wandering
the overgrowth. The trees are weighty
with fruit and possibility
and I just don't believe him.
This is not some desert mirage.
What I see, in fact, is
the opposite of fallow.
A matrix of earth and roots and all the good tools
for bearing fruit. Couldn't get any
better than this, I think,
the right shade, the right sun, rain,
all of it right and obviously more than enough.
The trees stand transcendent and wise,
and indeed, the branches climb higher
than I'll ever be.
A primal tangle of
bark and leaf and blossom, but mostly

what there is
is fruit.
Poised there like a studio photograph,
all luster and perfection,
something Mapplethorpe could have conjured
in his off-hours from the lilies.
The trees gratuitous,
gorgeous orbs of color, and the word "bounty"
is what springs to mind at a moment like this.
Or Eden. I am in
such a garden.
And yet.
Each thing I take, once opened,
reveals the true truth of itself.
Under shiny, promising skins,
the interiors have waged a losing battle.
Without fail
the plums and cherries are ruined microcosms of flesh,
the oranges hollow skeletons of their well-fed supermarket cousins.
The avocados have simply lied to themselves.
Inside their mottled moonscape shells
lies a fibrous wasteland of pit and disease.
I wonder how, with its fruit in such decline,
and a graveyard of castoffs haloing
underneath, like a perpetual, vicious reminder of
doom and genetic horticultural failure,
how a tree, nevertheless, can aim skyward
with such unstoppable abandon.

first love

In her mind's eye, she is perennially 12, eyeing the basketball court, white sneakers on parquet, shorts hugging her thighs, just before the shot clock begins, all that electric possibility. She is a dreamer yes, but there is a fierceness to this particular dream, a kind of clinging. Her body, fluid but precise, her legs purposeful, trustworthy. She was not a dancer, but underneath these fluorescent lights, before an accordion of bleachers, she could dance. She remembers the strides she took down-court. She remembers an animal certainty about where she needed to go for the shot. She remembers the ball like home, her body squaring to meet it.

You could say this was her first love, her first contact with something both outside and inside of herself. It was that kind of symmetry. It was that kind of longing. On Saturday mornings, when the games were held, she would arrive at the gym with a small tremble in her gut. The gym was large and loud. There were islands of chaos everywhere, but she steered through them. Game buzzers and referee whistles cut rudely through air, but she didn't hear them. She maneuvered through these minefields as if nothing in the world could touch her, and found a spot on the sidelines to tighten her laces until she could feel the tongue of the sneakers groove into the tops of her feet.

She remembers the smell of the waxed gym floor. She remembers the waistband of her shorts against her stomach. She remembers the burnt sienna of the basketball, its thin black stripes cutting into eighths. She remembers her hands like sticky tentacles. She remembers the freckles on her calves, the beginnings of hair on her shins and knees. She remembers the three blue stripes on the top of her socks. She remembers how hungry she was.

Twenty-five years later, she takes to the court like a cautious mother. There are others there, younger, sprightlier, braver than she. It is hard not to worry that she will get hurt. It is hard not to worry that she will get tired. It is hard not to notice the dim wash of pain in her hips, the hiccup of her legs. The sneakers are cement, trapping her ankles. Her shorts swallow her thighs. She is tall and exposed as willow tree. Now she notices everything - the hollow echoes of the gym, the harsh spotlight of the overheads, the heft of her opponent, and *she* has become the distraction, the perilous island she must navigate around, her body in a kind of raw anarchy, the parquet too slippery, a scene of possible disaster. But despite this, or perhaps because of it, her love stubborn and exquisite as ever.

everything new again
on the occasion of my nephew's birth

You have no idea what an airplane is
or what blue looks like
or how to tie shoes or unlock doors or break someone's heart.
You've entered as innocent as water, forgiving as the moon,
and looking at you I, too, can unremember the stars,
the view from Macchu Picchu, the shape of ferns
and triangles, the sticky taste of peanut butter, the smell
of a single lily in a glass vase.

Look how easily you've made
everything new again, and how deep
in the palm of your hand you hold the
tiniest bloom of a secret no one can know:
what will call to you to be touched,
to be held and kept close.

the view from 20D

Airborne again, Hartford to Dallas to home,
the lights of Santa Fe twinkling 32,000 feet below
and the exit row all to myself
which isn't a bad metaphor for the last week,
something opening, revealing itself,
the freedom to choose, to stay or to leave,
not the defeat I was thinking it to be,
the consolation prize, the last-ditch ditching,
but freedom, a clear exit row leading to the right wing
of this big, beautiful bird. On the phone two nights ago,
E said that it would be alright if it turned out
we needed to live apart, and it wasn't about the dogs
this time. She said it calmly, plainly, without controversy
or ugliness or as a substitute for I dare you or Do you love me.
Just an "if and then" scenario, a choice, the best kind
of freedom for a girl like me, clear exit row,
all the legroom in the world, and this is the only way
I can imagine sitting back and enjoying the flight.
All week, resting at my mother's,
the stretchy solitude, the night all mine, the light all mine
at the side of the bed and turned off at some ungodly hour
only when the jetlag and my mulchy mind finally
let me sleep, and I don't know how many times I turned over,
put hands behind my head, manipulated the pillows,
thought about her hand on my thigh, just lying there,
as if there was nothing else in the world we could be.
This is what good love does to you, lays its hands on you even
when it's not in the room, and this is why I can sit
in my exit row and not think about the sound the handle
would make if I pulled it, not think about the million pounds

of pressure, not rehearse a scene that features a perilous drop
to the bottom of the earth, the rush and catastrophe of
abandoning ship just when it's reached such a fine
cruising altitude. Instead, I am measuring the two hours
to go before the plane touches down again,
imagining the ginger ale she would have ordered,
the trashy magazine we would have ogled together,
the sun sinking down so fast but that solid palm on my thigh,
like good reason, like faith, like its own kind of forever.

a dime in the asphalt

It was a day to celebrate but you were so quiet,
eating your Cheerios as a new president took the stands,
your coffee cooling as words spread out into the freezing morning
over a million huddled close, waving their flags.
You felt disassembled, disembodied, not having slept
very well the night before (you told yourself) but really,
let's be honest here, you felt like you were just
missing the party, too far from the center of things, a negative
ion abandoned, inadvertently, by electrons, and that feeling
clutched at you all day, through a parade and scores of marching bands,
through hand-waving and photo opportunities and
evening gowns and first and last dances.
Maybe it will always be a little like this, you thought
on your way to the car after the sun went down.
Maybe you will never quite touch down into the nuclei
of crowds, never land dead center in a room where
the heat holds itself in the most, never get your lemon tree
to flourish on the back deck.
You will have your moments, of course.
You will feel a small glow in your solar plexus,
feel a lover's tongue on your neck, drink good wine
in front of a winter fire, have a strange dog nuzzle
your bent knees and eat from your open hands.
You will feel such luck, sometimes, the cables of a bridge
rising out of heavy fog, the road hugging your wheels
toward home. Sometimes, it will be slim, this light,
this window, this fragment of suspension. Sometimes,
it will be just a dime in the asphalt. It doesn't matter.
You will see yourself in that island of nickel and copper,
bordered on all sides by rock and gravity, and that will be enough.

You will lean down and reach for that bright coin,
tuck it in the right pocket of your jeans and think yourself
worthy of this tiny fortune, and know all at once you are proximate
to everything, even when you can't quite touch it.

phantom love

Take, for example, the little boy,
age 7, who told you raptly of the minor
characters in "The Night at the Museum,"
a movie you knew you would never see and yet,
which came alive in the boy's telling.

You fell in love with him, so briefly,
in the time it took to bend down
eye level with the DVD jacket he was holding,
you loved everything about him in just one minute,
the small gaps between his front teeth,
his sweet lisp, the mop of hair dropping
over his forehead, the way he launched so breathlessly
into the story.
The other day, you fell for the old man holding court
in front of the Walgreen's on Fillmore, his toothy grin,
his palm facing upward waiting for change. You loved
the way his eyes explored your face, how he really looked,
in the way few people do, in the dead center of you,
and you loved him for his bravery, for his honesty,
for the boldness in his question when he asked you
if you could spare anything.

Last month, it was the cashier at the Safeway
at the Red Hill Shopping Center, because she was
impatient and scrambling and looked on the verge
of emotional collapse, braids swinging violently
as she rang up your purchase. You fell for her
hardness, her upset, her bad customer service,
and you really caved in when out of nowhere,

after you asked her how her day was going,
she spilled the beans about her financial woes,
the full-time class load, the child at home,
the health insurance premiums going up, those rotten
scoundrels at corporate who were responsible
for dealing these blows, and all she needed was
$400 to get her through the month, and by God
she'd barely make it, three double shifts this week.
You couldn't help yourself then, all that trouble,
how you ached and loved and ached again.

You are so good at this, this phantom love,
this dalliance with affection and sympathy,
this earnest fidelity you dole out barely
blinking an eye, and there is even a kind of
swooning, a vertical fall to somewhere you
don't quite recognize yet feel so comfortable in.
You stand there, gluttonous with purpose,
your heart flying open, all that love pouring out,
bucketfuls, a whole galaxy, you are spilling over
with it, unabashedly, having forgotten yourself,
the frumpy minutiae of your day, your pasty-white
dissatisfactions. You let it all go like snowflakes,
like lint, like an afterthought, and fill yourself to brimming.
And it's strange how quickly you wanted to run this morning,
love's gaze right on you, persistent and real, the opposite
of the fleeting warmth you've given so recklessly
to the boy, the old man, the cashier - this love, instead, bright
and bold with promise, deep and searching and true
and oh, how you wanted to run. And maybe it's because sometimes
this kind of love is glaring and relentless and refuses
to leave, despite your best attempts to shatter it,

and you don't know what do to about that kind
of love, which is to say you don't quite know
what it means to stay stock-still and let love wrap around
you with its solid, warm wool. You don't quite know
how to bury your head in it and close your eyes
against its embrace. You don't quite know what it takes
to put your arms down and stop fighting.

tangerines

A wide green bowl of tangerines. Summer incarnate.
The June afternoon folding us in.
School had ended, or was just ending.
We lay horizontal on the carpet, inches from the kitchen,
sun tumbling through the window. We were luminous.
We had made love, or were just about to.
It didn't matter. The tangerines were plump and intact.
The sky was cloudless, betraying nothing.
To say I was overcome by beauty would be a lie.
No, I was resting in it. It surrounded me, a cocoon.
It was soft as cashmere. I was a baby, a bud,
a dandelion, a feather. You were so close
I could feel your hipbones. I was memorizing your eyebrows,
the arc of your thumbnail, the backs of your knees.
Nothing escaped me.
The bowl had been a gift. It was not quite circular.
There were small dips and rises in its construction.
It was an anomaly among the dishes.
It was not for salad, or spaghetti.
It was for tangerines.
The afternoon held us close, sun and love pinning us to the floor.
I was a wide green bowl.
We were not quite circular.
There were dips and rises in our construction.
You lay in my arms like a bird, like a single raindrop.
Like a tangerine.

breakfast: meditations on love

1.
Butter. Thick cuts of it into a pan.
Two eggs. A white bowl.
The kettle on.
Espresso teaspooned into a French press.
Twenty rotations of the wrist,
the eggs poured in.
And then, all of it, waiting.
It is a matter of time, of course,
but still. Waiting.
I am waiting.

2.
I do not want to order the complicated pancakes
with the sour cream batter and the stone fruit compote
or the omelet bulging at the seams
with a small farm of fall vegetables.
It's a shame. This restaurant is known for such specialties.
The chef has won praise in the local press,
a legion of devotees, a street named after him.
The tourists keep coming, the menu keeps growing,
the kitchen staff forced to keep up with the demand.

3.
My father was a magician with maple syrup.
He made it, from scratch, every Saturday morning,
while the French toast soaked in its egg bath.
Water, sugar, maple flavoring.
It took me years to realize this wasn't the real thing.

4.
New Year's Day. By the stove, a stack
of crepes. On the counter, smoked salmon,
three kinds of cream cheese, bagels,
fruit salad. Bottles of Prosecco chilling in the fridge.
I am ready.
In minutes, the house will be full of hungry bodies.
The disassembly will begin.

5.
When we drove across country, my sister and I disagreed
on only one thing.
She would rise, grumpy, not hungry at all.
I insisted
on breakfast.
While she sat and I ate, a silence swelled between us.

6.
On a friend's refrigerator door, family snapshots.
A magnetic alphabet. Drawings from preschool.
A shopping list. Coupons. A reminder from
the dentist. Birthday cards from a recent party.
On mine: a calendar too small to write on.
A schedule of gym classes
I have no intention of attending.

7.
My mother eats an apple every morning.
"I want to *be* an apple," she says,
and at first I'm confused because
the only words I can think of are "round"
and "easily bruised."

But then she elaborates.
It has something to do with the tree.

orange towels

Maybe they're too bright, not thick enough, a little on the cheap
side. But now, in the heart of summer, it's not just the weather
that's changed. Walking down the Target aisles, I keep
thinking about the house we lived in, the way we moved together
in the kitchen, in the yard, at night in bed. That day you brought
home the blue bath towels from Pottery Barn and I gulped at the price.
How we quarreled about the espresso machine, whether we ought
to get the really good one, or if a less chic version would suffice.

Later, we'd labor over the bureau, the rugs, even cheese and coffee,
and eventually, I learned to bite my tongue, accept the cost
of a life created by two instead of one. But something in me
balked and staggered, wanting something of simplicity, feeling lost
among the wealth of objects we accumulated. But this is not a poem
about haggling or household goods, because strolling down
the long, wide acreage of the store, I do feel a wash of wistfulness for the home
we made, took care of, loved and leaned into for comfort. And yet now,
unabridged, my eyes wander cartoonishly, carelessly, then land on an upper shelf
where a line of orange towels lie primped and plump, and the price
is right, and I'm no longer needful of sanction or approval if it's just myself,
fresh from a shower, dripping on the bathroom rug. So I don't think twice
about the purchase, and heave the towels into a bulging cartful of
things you would probably not approve of, and something in this act of defiance
reminds me of the ways you might have held yourself back too, the love
you gave in spite of yourself, how much you kept quiet to keep *my* alliance.
Are you feeling any freer now? Are you cleaving from our knitted past?
Are you grabbing back your life at last?

dressing up for the doctor
in memory of Danielle Drumke

Dr. Brown doesn't know I showered for her,
shaved my legs nice and smooth,
prepped and primped like I would
for a first date, scrubbed myself clean
of all possible unpleasantness, gave her
a fresh canvas to investigate on this
overcast day, a Thursday a little on the chilly side.
There's a part of me that believes
a good swipe with the washcloth
and fresh underwear will give me
the clean bill of health I'm after,
because there's something altogether mystical
about how one person can escape an early mortality
and another can fall headfirst into the flames.

When I was nearing 30, I ran into a woman
I knew on the 5th floor of the medical center
on a university campus in San Francisco. I was
leaving from my annual Pap smear. She was
visiting her oncologist. She was 27. She had brain cancer,
some crazy thing, stage 4. She was on her way out,
although no one would have known it then, all smiles,
looking like she owned the world, like it was hers
to play with, like she wasn't about to let anything pass her by.

Less than two years later she would be gone,
permanently, and I'm thinking of her now
as I spread my legs for the good Dr. Brown,
realizing that smooth legs and an even bikini line

are of little consequence in this examining room,
that I could just as easily be dangling into the pit
of some irreversible horror.
And yet, this is no way to keep breathing, as if any moment
life could topple and shatter, as if I am just squeaking by.
Even when she had it worst, Danielle managed to fly home
for Thanksgiving, take a trip to New Zealand, visit friends
in Seattle, and in all those pictures she is grinning, looking
like she hit the jackpot, like she was made of luck.
She must have had her moments, I'm sure,
the derisions at God, some inflammatory assault
into her bathroom mirror, watching her scalp
metastasize, the long shoe-horn scar biting
her skin, disrupting the symmetry of her body
and everything else she had to cleave from -
a spot on the soccer team, playing drums for the band,
a lover who couldn't take it when things got bad,
the surgeries and speech loss and a wheelchair
and hospice. But in her photographs she is
the brightest light in the room, a star,
a goddess, a golden opportunity.

The ovaries look good, Dr. Brown says,
kneading her hands on my lower abdomen.
Perfectly normal, she adds, and even she looks relieved,
and for a moment I forget what a narrow escape this could be,
a momentary lapse on the part of the Fates,
who are off somewhere else wreaking their havoc.

For a moment I gaze down on my body and see
something long and beautiful and intact,
a smooth stretch of highway heading into

the deep, wild heart of the universe,
and there is nothing else to do
but say thank you.

freethrow

Coming home from a loss,
the semifinal basketball game
that could have been a sweet victory
had the final seconds played out differently.
We'd been ahead for most of it,
plunking down the key rebounds,
and these funky shots which somehow
wound their way in.
But our poor showing on the freethrow line,
in the end, cost us the game.

This could be about underwhelming
shooting percentages and the reliable left-
hand hook of mine which, for once,
didn't cooperate. I could grouse about that, or
about the way my stomach hurt from eating too soon
before the game even started,
a full meal that should have waited. Or I could
go on about unfairness and what I believed in my heart
we had earned, a season of showing
up and working together and blah blah blah.
I could plea in this poem for something
better next time, or talk about lost chances
and bitter ends and why nothing's fair even when
you want it badly enough.
But what I want to tell you is this:

How long those last seconds were,
a beautiful ache of time,
as if God were gently pushing thumbs on a clock's hands,

slowing down the spinning earth
just for us, just here, in the fertile air
of the gym on a Tuesday night,
our high-topped feet all planted on the same parquet floor
and what a gift that was
time slowing down
feet planted on the same floor
and the lungs working
and all eyes on the ball.
And something about the gym, too,
the safety there,
this reprieve from everything else that wasn't safe,
which barely needs mentioning but
there was luck there, too,
for the reprieve,
even as the seconds dwindled and there was no
miracle three-pointer at the buzzer
and we went home without the trophy.
Luck in those final moments, I felt it,
the strange sensation of hope
passing through on its way
to somewhere else.

how to start over

1.
Resist the temptation to wipe the slate clean entirely.
You cannot do this.
You are where you are.
But you can dust. You can mop. You can cleanse your belly
of all the heavy cheeses you ate at last month's holiday parties.
You can initiate the day with decaf.
You can rake four batches of leaves from the lawn.
You can sing, loudly, in the car to no one
but the man on the radio who is singing with you.
You can decide that the apple pie you are craving
will not come from your hands, your oven, your kitchen,
but from the bakery aisle at your neighborhood grocery.

2.
Ignore the titles from the self-help shelves and glossy
women's magazines, with their sound bytes of colorful insight.
You do not need a makeover, a diet, a religious conversion.
You do not need to get more in touch with your feelings.
You do not need potassium, or St. John's Wort, or a colonic.
You need a walk, communion with shore birds, a rainstorm,
a glass of wine in front of a fire, lip-gloss, a whole evening
of the novel you read only incrementally, at night, before bed.

3.
Ignore the calendar, the clock, the larger itineraries
ticking their niggling bits of time.
You will sleep when you need to.

You will know when it is time for water, for a shower,
for a phone call, for a kiss, for solitude, for Indian food,
whatever nourishment you need for your throat, your ears,
the palms of your hands, the hunger just under your skin.

4.
Imagine, despite your unbearable faults and fissures,
You are still a thing of beauty, a rare creature, a snowflake,
a singular, spectacular atom circumnavigating the tangled astronomy
of your life the only way you know how.

clover

It grew, without intervention, in the front yard,
despite the less-than-fertile soil, despite the first
unexpectedly arid weeks of autumn, despite the garden's
dangerous proximity to a litter-strewn street,
despite dog droppings and sticky sap, despite
telephone wires and a carpet of fallen foliage left
to rot and disappear into obsolescence.
And yet, unaided, unwatched, untended,
the clover insisted, answering this spectacular neglect
with a steady, steely patience, waiting
for a rare rain or the fickle generosity
of a stranger emptying the last inches from an old water bottle.
So now, November, and an anachronism of spring
has sprung. What was barren has entered into the thick
of an immaculate conception. Something fleshy is on the verge,
sprouting its bright green wings.

I don't know how long you will stay close,
warming my skin with yours, breathing into me
your moist and swirling air.
But I am certain that even this brief oxygen
will be enough.

flight

It's not that the plane is crowded or that you will be stuck in it for the next 10 hours or that you will not sleep because of the crying baby three rows up or the cramped seat or the fact that you simply never sleep on planes because of the twisted anxiety-fantasy you have that your help will be needed in an emergency and you will be one of the few people calm enough to do so, will have your wits about you, will know how to activate the exit-row doors and help the elderly out of the seatbelts and into the evacuation slide.

It's not the one wobbly overhead compartment and the strange noise coming from the engines or the flight attendants' falsely cheery faces or the lack of general ventilation or the tight quarters of the bathrooms and the unreasonable fear you have that the bathrooms at the end of the plane, could fall off in a heartbeat.

It's not the occasional turbulent patches or that you will be flying with no visible land mass beneath you or your general lack of understanding all these years about how planes even work, how an aircraft carrying more than 300 bodies and God-knows-how-many thousands of tons of cargo manages to stay aloft in the first place.

What it is is that there's a man sitting one row back and to your right who is frantically, obsessively swaying back and forth, rubbing his hands over his forehead, looking skyward and chanting what sounds like a rush of Arabic because you think you hear the word "Allah" a couple of times, and as the plane takes off, the man's voice rises in pitch and intensity, and his eyes roll back into his head and his whole body shudders epileptically, and suddenly he grabs for something in his front shirt pocket, something in a small round tin box, which he clutches to his face and rubs into his cheeks, and there's more chanting, more chanting and eyes rolling heavenward, and you have no idea what's in the box, or what he is getting so feverish about, this ever-so-slight wailing erupting from him, and you look to your left at your lover who is calmly reading the dinner menu and adjusting the overhead fan, and your mind races to a moment that may or may not come, and you wonder if you have it in you to wrestle an old man to the ground, plying from him the piece of business he holds in his hand. You wonder if you could throw yourself to a task like that, disarming a dangerous stranger spouting Arabic to the heavens, and most of all you wonder if you will recognize the moment if it comes, when the balance will tip enough to force you into action, when the chanting, rocking man will leap out of his seat and do something to change your life forever.

But then the plane stops climbing and levels at last, and the dense white clouds are far below, all those miles already behind you, and everything just pure blue sky now, the engines relaxing into a hum, the baby nursing or asleep, and the man with the tin box and the heavenward eyes and the urgent Arabic is now adjusting his earphones and tuning in to *Shrek 2*, which is to say he is no longer posing an immediate threat, because his arms are lying still on his lap and he is silent, his small tin package disappearing back into his shirt pocket. You see the small bulge there, an outline of silver metal tucked away behind a film of Egyptian cotton and you think about the green glass ring you have brought on board, this augury of safe passage you always carry, which you have secreted away during takeoff in the palm of your hand. You think about the small prayers you have released in tight and dangerous spaces, the fibrillating pleas you have uttered into the darkness, what you have clutched to your body in your hour of need, every bargain you have struck with God to keep you awake and alive and here for another day, and then another.

instantaneous

It will not serve you to wait, to linger idly
by the window counting the lines
in your left hand or the loose change
in your fringed front pocket. It will not make you wiser
to consider the plodding of the shore birds
or the summery grin of an ice cream truck rounding
the final corner in your neighborhood. You will not be
more beautiful in the nuanced light of dinner candles
or the vertical plunge of a dark red dress. The moon
will not wait for you. The sun is impatient as ever.
Yes, there is something purposeful about clutching
your moments like so much sand, small granular spectacles
to examine and forage for their glinty promise.
But let me tell you: it is not the same as living.

Come. Follow this imperfect, furtive day
into a sooty downtown street.
You will not see the beautiful
black man selling jewelry, or hear
the island song he sings under his breath.
You will not distinguish the five-dollar bill
centrifuged in the subway grate,
or the poem you might have written about
the single-footed seagull swimming in tossed breadcrumbs
had you seen it in time.
Instead, you will look up at some precise second,
the hot zenith of noon barreling down, nearly blinding you,
and the dumb luck of your next breath will land squarely, instantaneous,
into the palm of your heart, flooding your whole world with green.

substitutes

When I want to remember I am not alone,
apple cobbler.
When I want to act like a teenager, or a kindergartner,
throw fists against a pillow,
four double-chocolate Milanos.
When I want to know that God is listening,
Earl Grey with honey and cream.
When I want to forget the argument,
cucumber, sliced on the diagonal.
When I am ready to face the fear,
lemons.
When I want your teeth in my neck,
a rib-eye steak.
When I am ready to say goodbye,
cast one last glance before the daisies fall,
Montefalco at the kitchen window.
When I want to swim the wide channel,
stay parallel to shore,
a fistful of grapes, a thick wedge of Manchego.
When I want silence,
a glass of Armagnac.
When I want noise,
two raspberry-peach Cosmopolitans.
When I am tired,
cold milk, cornflakes in the orange bowl.
When I am impatient,
tangerines.
When I want to make everything disappear,
climb back into the womb,
a trip to Mitchell's for mint chip.

When I want the moon a little closer,
carrot-ginger soup, a dollop of sour cream,
an intimate pinch of chives.
When the light is too much to bear,
scrambled eggs, wheat toast, apricot preserves.
When I've had enough of the rollercoaster,
the ache of the climb, the precipitous pitch into the abyss,
ice water, grapefruit, multivitamins.
When I want to start over,
white rice and butter.
When I couldn't be happier,
wild salmon, fresh ginger, radishes.
When I miss my mother,
broth, maple yoghurt, sautéed cauliflower, unsalted almonds.
When I miss my father,
Rainier cherries, roast potatoes, fried chicken,
a single square of dark chocolate.
When I miss myself,
tomatoes, mozzarella, basil,
drop after drop of olive oil.

life lessons from the street musicians

The man playing drums outside the Ferry Building
was not asking for change. Instead, he kept time
on a makeshift snare, a collection of empty buckets
turned on their heads, little tin pans alongside, and bells
strapped to his feet. A handwritten sign out front spoke of his defiance.
"In these tough times," it said, "I refuse to accept defeat."
And thus the man carved beats out of the early Saturday morning.
The music did not criticize the economy, or his bad luck
on the job market, or the string of misfortunes getting in the way
of health and fiscal happiness. Instead, it shouted its joy into the air,
punctuating the footsteps of everyone within earshot -
the bright-eyed tourists, the sweaty joggers, the wild-haired women
selling cheap jewelry, the homeless, the waitress on her way
to the lunch shift, the meter maid, the fortune teller with her
worn tarot deck, the cab driver punching in his first cup of coffee,
the parents juggling twins in a double-wide stroller, the boy
biting into his first summer peach. The music landed on everything
it touched. And it was impossible not to get swept up, too, to start to believe
I had an equal power to ward off the dissonant assaults of the day.
The man did not see me reach in my pockets, nor did he see
the coins I slid his way, but I understood. This kind of music
requires full attention, and he had to keep playing.
So the song stayed where it was, inside the drummer man,
but the echo his hands made couldn't contain itself,
its sweet rebellion following me home.

suddenly, an orchard

You knew about the apple tree.
You saw its fruit, poignant on the branches.
You had walked the teeming carpet
of the fallen on the way to get your laundry. You had seen
where the worms had had a field day. You had shaken
the knobby limbs for your young nephew, watched his delight
as a shower of gold fell to the earth. You had bent down to eat
with him. You had imagined a pie, bubbling in the oven.
You had purchased a sachet of cinnamon. You had remembered
the dozen autumns you'd spent in New England, the apple trees there
prophesying the inevitable coming of cold, the stillness of snow,
your necessary hibernation. You had pointed to the solid trunk,
reclining in your deck chair, exclaimed over your luck -
a fruit-bearing tree in your own backyard! In the city, to boot! -
and let the thought slide over you at night, the reign of this tree
like a kind of safe harbor, the comfort of this
prosperous landscape rustling just outside your windows.
You were so enamored with the very *idea* of that tree,
it became the only thing you saw, and felt, and understood.
It was what you turned to when you pictured the prized
green lot that was your backyard. It was what you said
when someone asked you about the house -
"And there's an apple tree!" you'd exclaim with the same
pink-cheeked wonderment you'd once given the treasure
found under your pillow the next morning after a tooth
was reclaimed by fairy hands. Your heart became filled
with that tree, your body aligned with its stature,
its wide reach skyward, its delicate balance of
flesh and wood - you saw yourself in all of it.

How you missed the plums is beyond you.
Perhaps you thought them rooted elsewhere,
a neighboring garden, the lucky stranger adjacent.
Perhaps you didn't know them as plums,
distinguished only a blur of red from the camouflage of branches,
an afterimage following the bright clutch of apples
in your foreground. Maybe you couldn't hold the possibility
they might have been gifted to you, too, having learned the art
of not wanting too much.

So it was only yesterday, looking for a friend's lost cat,
slinking into the further reaches of your garden and mewling
into the advancing evening, that you saw that other tree.
Your eyes were cocked earthward for a flicker of tail, a quick dart
of flank, and your gaze landed instead on a perfect circle of plums,
tiny, unblemished, ripe as a kiss, and all at once the view changed.
You looked up, and suddenly,
an orchard.

a short letter to an old love

Forgive me my viciousness,
my name-calling, my absent-minded
mishaps, my cruelties and calamities,
and all the ways we fumbled while I fled.
Forgive me my anger, my flight,
my bad timing, my ill-conceived attempts
at disappearing, my slipping into any available
porthole to get a little bit of air.
Forgive me my haste, my impatience,
my mess, my chaotic heart.
Forgive me my clumsiness while
you fell, unattended,
into the busy, dirty street.
I didn't know how to say it
at the time, and even now
any word between us is a monster
crawling out of a still febrile cave,
a great roiling of bat wings.
It's just that our hands
couldn't fit together,
that's all.

strand

Last night, a single strand of her hair
surfaced on my pillow. All day, on the boat,
as I tried righting myself on water skis, and failing,
I had begun to convince myself
that whatever momentum that had carried us all year
was beginning to sputter and topple.
I gripped the rope as if my life
depended on it, and still, it flew out of my hands.
On deck she was as beautiful as ever. It was not hard
to keep falling in love. When she took to the wakeboard,
her skin gleaming in the Delta sun,
it was almost heartbreaking how easy it looked.
She was floating. She was an angel.
I wanted to dive in after her like a dolphin, follow her trail.
I couldn't.

After all of my attempts to rise above the surface,
I was shivering wildly, my hands
reddened and sore. I climbed into my towel and stayed there,
head down, legs goose-pimpled. She rubbed my back
as if I were a child.
I was.
I told myself it would always be like this,
me trying to hold on to such an unwieldy ride, and she
already aloft and steady, eyes pinching the horizon.
When I came home, I thought,
Maybe this is the beginning of the end, and I began
the terrible act of curling back inside myself,
reeling my heart back in, stowing my memories in the dark.
But no.

I pulled back the cover of my bed, and there it was.
A strand of her, a slim remainder,
a micron of her body resting squarely
where her head had been just last week,
as I lay against her on a Tuesday afternoon.
And I knew
that something of her was still with me,
singing me to sleep.

luck and other variables

You were not on that SamTrans bus heading down 280
that caught fire after a late-morning collision
with the blue Corolla. You did not have to be
snapped out of your seatbelt by a frantic passenger
when you turned, white-faced, away from the flames.
You were not rushed in a racing ambulance to San Francisco General,
where surgeons worked on your body, doing their best
to piece you back together.
Neither were you on the bridge in Minneapolis when it collapsed,
sending its human cargo tipping into a gape-mouthed river.
You were not in a Utah mine, breathing your last hours in darkness.
You were not in a 12-seat chopper screaming toward Afghanistan.
You were not caught, held, lied to, raped, distorted into death.

You were somewhere suburban, ticking off your shopping list,
returning the late videos and stopping for ice cream.
Or, having decided to let rush hour do its thing without you,
you left the house at 8:30 instead of 8, and got to
squeeze by the blackened wreckage on the side of the freeway.
You were watching television, listening to the radio, reading the paper.
You were lucky, or late, or 6,000 miles away,
or born in the wrong decade, or a red-haired woman,
or near-sighted, or left-handed, or in the bathroom, or something else.
But another was not spared these small discrepancies, and for that
you are wringing your hands in disbelief, and a sadness
you don't quite know what to do with but hold, like a tiny broken bird,
close to your hot cheek, your dark blue veins,
your stubborn, indefensible aliveness.

with the wineglass almost empty

I am looking at the moon's slow rise
above this city, this windswept hill,
this winding block, this square house,
this little body breathing, unselfconsciously,
into the final stretch of evening. I want
to pray correctly to such a gift, fold hands
together with discrete reverence, bend slight as a breeze
to the window and send a soft song through the glass.
I want to remember how fragile and perfect time is,
how the world's furious moments can fall into a lake-calm,
how clouds like flour can dust even the dirtiest passage,
how the heart can curve into a conch shell,
echo wetly and warmly the ocean it came from.
Love, your fingertips have been here, your lips
a stain of easy welcome, something of my body
imprinted with yours, our various surfaces colliding.
The way we cup around each other like circles.
The duvet of cheek against cheek. The giggle of eyelashes.
How I have begun to taste you even in sleep,
a single bud-drop expanding on my tongue,
sweeter than anything that came before it.

how to get everything you've ever wanted

First, you must believe yourself worthy.
This is not the same as deserving.
This is not a promotion, a raise, a graduation.
This is not the prize you win after countless attempts at winning.
This is you standing naked in an empty house at midnight,
the street below dark and silent, the fruit bowl in your kitchen
brimming with oblong shapes that eventually you recognize
as bananas. This is you aligning yourself with the stationary and the shifting:
the broken light bulb, the foghorn, the water tower, the power cord,
the orange chair you write in, the carpet stain that won't disappear,
the sound of morning cars on Guerrero, the swaying palm tree, the laces
on your basketball shoes, a stack of paper, a water bottle snapped to your bike,
a piece of lint your lover removes from your cheek, that cheek, that lover,
the new blossoms on the lemon tree, the toilet that needs to be flushed twice,
the grooves on the coffee table, a calculator that needs only sunlight
to turn it on, the man who cuts your hair, his pierced lip, his quick scissors,
the letters your grandfather sends, the gas pump, neon, frozen waffles,
a stack of martini glasses, doorways, picture frames, kitchen remodels,
long white envelopes bulging with receipts, a backpack filled with dirty gym clothes,
an apple tree in hibernation, empty check boxes, the steps outside City Hall,
a balloon escaping the clutch of a 3-year-old, tears barreling down her cheeks,
an anchor, a crossing guard, a detour, a yield sign poised on the lip of the highway.
Forget the pulverizing mirror, that blistering microscope of discrepancy.
You are not less than but equal to.
Throw away the movie reel casting you as the villain, the buffoon, the mistake.
You are not less than but equal to.
Turn from the narrow dead-end road book-ended by barbed wire.
You are not less than but equal to.
When he tells you you're beautiful, say thank you.
When she holds your hand driving across the bridge, say yes.

When the morning opens, say hello.
When the light flickers out, say sleep.

dayenu

If only for this plank of deck.
If only for this arrow of sun.
If only for this cup of flour, this couch cushion, this arch in the foot.
If only for eight in the evening.
If only for a measure of drumbeats.
If only for a dab of cold water on the face.
If only for yesterday.
If only for never.
If only for "how are you" and "come here" and "please."
If only for an hour's nap, a scattering of birdseed, a full rotation of gears.
If only to remember the letters of my first alphabet.
If only for the deepening lines in my forehead.
If only for scars, for errors in judgment, for leaps of faith, for intuition,
for fresh footfalls on an old path.
If only for a river of insects, electrified by early summer.
If only for the outline of mountain, the sketch of a word,
the thinnest suggestion of moon.
If only for pound cake, for a flat of strawberries,
a stiff wedge of cheese, a glass of pink lemonade.
If only for thirst.
If only for sleep.
If only for death.
If only for a climb to the waterfall, a clutch of fur in a pine tree,
a story, a fable, a dream.
If only for the pit of one mango.
If only for a splinter.
If only for a soft hand on a sore shoulder.
If only for a purple shawl over an old bureau, a box of yellow tablets,
a haircut, a hiccup, a headache.
If only for a dim but precise memory.

If only for lost and tragic language.
If only for an unsent letter, or too many letters.
If only for a late-night dance.
If only for a lie.
If only for the long and lonely walk home.
If only for a clatter of seabirds, the first bubble of coffee,
If only for drowsy, for hungry, for can't get enough.
If only for love.
If only for stones skipping across a pond.
If only for a narrow light in the hallway at midnight.
If only for a single, slippery yes.

I must offer myself.
Whole, shattered, fleshy,
full of disaster and ache and fury and spectacular neglect.
Here is a thing of beauty. I must take it.
Here is a thing of sorrow. I must take it.
Here is a body in all its innocence and failure. I must take it.
Here is a raw heart, breaking but alive.
I must stay close. Somewhere a piece of music is buried in the rubble,
a steam of fresh bread rising from the oven,
a sliver of dust flying toward the stars.

believe

Maybe the camera crew is at someone else's house,
a spotlight haloing over another's fleshy story.
Maybe the mailman is delivering the good news
to your neighbor, or a different city entirely,
and you come home to a rash of catalogues,
the second notice for a doctor's bill, a plea
from the do-gooders for whatever you can spare.
Maybe you haven't cleaned your kitchen floor in weeks,
forgotten to nourish the front garden, spilled too much
coffee in your car, weaving through traffic.
Maybe you are 10 pounds heavier than last year.
Maybe your skin is betraying your age.
Maybe winter is ravaging your heart.
Maybe you are afraid, or lonely, or furious, or wanting out
of every commitment you entered with such vigor and trust.
Maybe you've bitten your nails down to the quick,
chosen your meals badly, ignored the advice of those
who know you best. Maybe you are stubborn as a toddler.
Maybe you are clumsy or foolish or hasty or reckless.
Maybe you haven't read all the books you're supposed to.
Maybe your handwriting is still illegible after all these years.
Maybe you spent too much on a pair of shoes you didn't need.
Maybe you left the window open and the rain ruined the cake.
Maybe you've destroyed everything you've ever wanted to save.
Still.

If anything, believe in your own strange loveliness.
How your body, even as it stumbles, angles for light.
The way you hold a dandelion with such yearning and tenderness,
the whole world stops spinning.

something for everyone

I want the water to fill your glass the moment
it sees your thirst.
I want the staircase to meet your footfalls.
I want the line to the freeway to move like breath.
I want the wind flattering your hairline, the rain shower
a welcome refreshment. I want the parking space to fit your car.
I want the birds on your back deck to warble in the exact way
they did during your childhood. I want the photographs
of all your holiday dinners buzzing with a certain unnamable
happiness. I want the dry cleaners to understand
your outrageous requests.
I want the man calling your house to survey
your thoughts on phone companies to remember
the evening is precious as silk. I want your new jeans to not
come undone in the wash. I want snow to land on your eyelashes
like it does in the movies, an etheric, slow-moving kiss.
I want a letter to arrive the moment
you feel most unwelcome of your own company.
I want the scent of lemons in the air. I want the power lines
overshadowed by the view your neighborhood offers at twilight.
I want the downtown ice rink to keep your fantasies aloft.
I want the moon to articulate your most punishing silence.
I want the willow tree revived and teeming, the broken daisies
resurrected and obstinate with brightness.
I want the labyrinth of what ifs narrowed
to a single, poignant sentence.
I want the tulips to be wild as clover, as fog, as good intentions.
I want your heart to cut through its own brutality,
for your body to see everything about you that's beautiful.
I want love to come at you in thick pats of butter,

in strands of spun sugar, heavy and light as cream.
I want it to bathe your skin until you are nothing
but forgiveness, until your shadows have disappeared,
until all of your perfect right angles have collapsed,
until you are a curve of a curve,
and your hands slide forward and open
and are able, at last, to feel everything.

strong

You don't have to be as strong
as you think you do.
You can come limping up the stairs,
stagger into my kitchen for water
and drink it as indelicately as a toddler,
and I will gaze at you with the same wonder
that broadsided me when I first realized
I could love you.

It does not matter if you are lost, or sick, or scared,
if the words you utter are gibberish or song,
if waking up makes your hair look funny,
if you forget the keys, if you burn our dinner,
if disaster is your ally.
You can enter my house like an elephant,
leave dirty handprints against the wall,
chew the mint directly off its pot
and I would whisper your name
like the caress it always is.

Love, I will falter too.
I will drive down a street that says
"Do Not Enter" and I will have missed the sign.
I will bump tender hips into the sharp corners
of every piece of furniture in the house
and curse louder than necessary.
I will make irreversible errors,
clutter the countertop with my messy heart,
leave wounds brutal and bleeding.
I will not fold the laundry into neat corners.

I will step haphazardly into a field of nettles.
I will almost ruin myself to catch you for the split second
you are catchable.

We don't have to be as strong
as we think we do.
If we wanted, we could fall
as easily as plastic soldiers.
We could slide our feet into the gutter
and wait for the rain,
sit so still our breath would sound
like a waterfall miles away.
If we wanted, we could unmake the plans
that married us to safety.
We could take the next exit
instead.
We could feed the world with our spectacular frailty.
We could start all over again.
We could let the glass shatter
into sand.

empty
for my brother

I can imagine your hands, tight against the bathroom walls,
water hammering the sink.
Maybe this is the only place you allow yourself the luxury
of desperation.
Then, inevitably, you leave the door behind,
and each hour piles up like a sword pointing at your gut.
Like the Gladiator you are,
you try to keep up with the carnage.

Last week, we sat on the couch in your living room
and I could feel how tired you were,
something in you heavy and flagging,
but still you stretched your lanky arms around my back
until they gathered me in full, and you were 10 again,
or I was, and I forgot what the story was.
And yet, the narrative insists on telling itself,
and days later it was this embrace that I forgot.
You were careening through so many cracks,
it would have been an act of military precision
not to fall.
Of course, by now, you are only trying to outrace
yourself.

Brother, if I could do anything,
I would take you to the Sierra road I saw this morning,
show you how after so many hours of snowfall,
everything had disappeared - the 18-wheelers' chain marks,
the tracks of the highway patrol cars barring the smaller exits,
even (I am guessing) the carcasses of winter creatures

darting across for home.
All of it empty, wiped clean of noise and mud and ruin,
with nothing but the invitation to come closer.
Even if what would come was pain or heartache or failure,
nevertheless a road, hushed, laid bare,
waiting for you to take it.

what brings you to the next morning

Maybe someone sang you to sleep.
Or there was a blackout, and you couldn't articulate
the hand in front of you.
Maybe the bedroom floor was a deserted beach,
your house a moonscape of solitude.
Or clothes had spilled like a rude volcano,
wine glasses from dinner scattered
on the coffee table and stained with lipstick,
still holding a thimbleful of revelry.
It could have been one of those nights you needed something
you couldn't name, a close-knit warmth, a Kleenex,
moisturizer, a lullaby cradling your eyelids.
Or else you were claustrophobic from attention,
the hairs on your arm standing on edge, rebellious,
your body tired of life under a microscope
and something of you desperate for escape,
anonymity, a Yosemite field in the thick of winter,
some carcass of a campsite where you could start again,
build your own small, unseen fire.
Maybe you were stranded in between, your heart caught
on some fishing line, half of you wanting a kitchen stool
to lean against, the other half wildly unfamiliar with the act
of staying still.

What I want to know
is what brings you to the next morning.
How you open one sleepy eye after the other,
part the Red Sea of your comfort and let the air,
graceless and obstinate, pull you into the day.
How you accept the hand that may offer either feather

or thistle. You ask for nothing, not a promise
or a warning or a little party celebrating your entrance,
and instead you heave your weariness from the room,
gather your limbs to the center, and rise.
Tell me what keeps you from plummeting backward.
Tell me on what hidden plume of air you allow yourself
that slim caesura of trust.
Tell me the story of your great impossible hope.
Tell me how your face tilts,
squinting for light.

the luxury of failure

After the cake had fallen.
After the vase shattered and the vacuum had died.
After she had miscalculated how much water
even the cactus needed. After a poem
had slipped through her fingers.
After she had broken someone's heart.
After the taxman had taken her savings and the rain
had wiped out the garden. After the apology
didn't come. After no one noticed her new dress.
After her body became a series of disappointments.
After she had run out of ways to save him and the cord
of her bedside lamp had frayed beyond repair.
After the bolts of the garage door had buckled
under the weight. After she had buried her wild anger.
After the doctors had reached an impasse.
After the weather showed no signs of improvement.
After the coffee failed to revive and the stranger
did not rescue her from loneliness. After desire
had not met with fulfillment. After the moon had
winked out and the sky became a wail of question marks.
After the detour had ended in a mud puddle.
After the horse would not come to feed at her hands.
After the baby refused to be held. After the tear
in her shirt had widened irreparably and the muscle for patience
had exhausted itself. After she could hold her breath
no longer. After winter had pummeled her with frost.
After the hill proved too much for her bicycle.
After the front door swelled and stuck and the window
was a cemetery of moths. After the wind
swallowed her whole. After love was a carpet

of potholes. After even escape eluded her.

She did not despair but instead
welcomed the luxury of failure,
the velvet of it warming her skin,
how easy it was to slide into its open arms,
and nestle against its breast.
She thought it would take everything she knew
to fling her weight against it, shoulder it
from her path, sandbag the corners of her house
to keep it from leaking in and drowning the furniture.
She imagined its animal clutch at her throat,
the feral mewling in her ear, the cadaver scent
of it putrefying the air. She had pictured
its hulking footsteps forecasting an earthquake ruin
for what she had worked so hard to keep whole.
She had armed herself against the possible wreckage,
kept the medicine cabinet replete with bandages,
left a surreptitious trail of breadcrumbs behind her.

But no.
It turned out failure
was a tiny slip of a thing,
a drop of water that could topple
an army,
a single seed offering this magnificent invitation:
Again.
Begin again.

poem after surgery

Tablespoons of chocolate pudding.
Gospel music slicing through rain.
Tabloid literature on the coffee table.
Three o'clock in the morning and still awake.
A bright red shirt.
A new pair of walking shoes.
Sex.
Avocados.
Tomato soup.
The two blocks to the train.
The sound of the doorbell.
The heady smell of the cheese shop.
Laughter.
An oval tablet four times a day.
Glasses and glasses of water.
A vase of orange tulips winking open.
The careful art of bathing.
A scar you already love.
Pomelos in the green bowl.
The cry of a distant ambulance.
Scavengers rummaging the recycling.
The twinkle of glass.
The deck, sodden and gleaming.
Dreams of swimming and giant movie theaters.
Your father, the evening before departure.
The heft and softness of his shoulders.
Your mother, fixing up a salad.
The slow peeling of bandages.
Tea.
The back of the woman you love.

Her fingers threading your hair.
A slim filament of moonlight.
Slippers.
The slide toward sleep.
You could start anywhere.
Start here.
Because you know
nothing
will be the same again.
And you know the body
is just the beginning.
Small acts of redemption are hiding
where you least expect them,
inkling seeds burgeoning in the dark soil,
an unseen greening,
in you and out of you,
even if you can't quite bring yourself
to believe it. Believe it.
All that is alive, alive, alive.
And there is no choice now
but to walk into that life,
that infinitesimal,
unfathomable geography,
and allow yourself
at last
to be healed.

let it be now

A trail of orange maggots feasting on your potted plants.
The paint peeling from a gap in the walls where rain
rudely sidled in. Dust camouflaging the top of your bureau.
Mail like the Leaning Tower of Pisa. A poem
at a standstill, your words like dough deprived of yeast.
The collision of artifacts in your garage.
Sunlight decimating the butter dish.
The closet bulging at the seams.
Your heart, an obstacle course of apology and need.
The front door swollen at the corners.
Laundry from your trip barring the beeline to bed.
A freezerful of meals you'll never eat.
Your mind a hamster wheel of what ifs.
The mirror wagging her finger at your deficits.
The way you hum yourself to sleep
with your catalog of solitudes.
The broken handle, spent light bulb, unsalvageable
zipper, cracked dishware, dismantled belief,
hope hiding under a thick blanket of complaint.
How you accumulate what needs discarding.
How you forgive what needs to witness pain.
Loss disguising as regret, yearning masking as contentment.
A stain you scrub until your hands are raw.
Shoes too precipitous for the long city blocks.
The toaster that keeps burning your breakfast.
Fault lines of an earthquake you know is coming.
How you shoulder against sadness. The lies
you tell to gloss over your rubble. The pair
of pants you are safeguarding in the closet
when your body decides, for once, to cooperate.

The stories of your heroic triumph or tragedy.
The dark sky you hold back with the fluorescent glare
of your kitchen. The pages of the book
you fall asleep to but never finish.
The dull newsreel rolling in your mind.
All that evidence of your unmagnificent living.

When are you going to put it all down?
When will you pluck yourself from under the terrible spotlight
you insist on training your disrepair, your unfinished business?
When will you refuse your own brutality?
When will you decide each chapter of your feeble existence
has exhausted itself of endings?

Let it be now.
Let this unheralded night signal
the death of your diminishment.
Let this unremarkable hour
celebrate the close
of every incompletion.
Let this ordinary moment deliver amnesty
from your imprisonment.
Let your body open
to the freedom it can't even begin
to imagine.

the beauty of grief

No one knows she cried her eyes out three days ago,
sat in her desk chair and wept, unable to see the screen.
No one knows how harshly she spoke to herself, flagellated
her already fragile spirit, lay on her bed with her forearms
pinching her eyelids flat, and made mad proclamations
against her weak, fractured heart. No one knows the hours
she's devoted to circling her sadness like a vulture,
the mileage she's worn into her soles, walking the hills of her city
in a series of unsuccessful attempts at forgetting.
No one heard the keening in the shower, or the thud
of her fists against the dashboard. No one saw
the resignation of her shoulder blades against the back door,
or her palms curling under the kitchen faucet as hot water
eviscerated the dishes, or the half-moons of mascara
threatening stains on the duvet and her favorite t-shirt.
There are no witnesses to the indentation
her back made on the couch, reeling from the storm,
no audience for the unsent letters pleading her cause, no bleacher
of cheerleaders as she made herself breakfast, in spite of the great effort
it took to crack eggs, spread hard butter on thin toast.
No one knelt before her dabbing a cold cloth on her forehead,
or fed her spoonfuls of oatmeal, or kneaded the soft
tissue of her lower back as she bent, again and again,
to heave trouble out of her way.

She had convinced herself of her own ruin,
a fault line splitting her body in two.
Her lungs felt thin as moth wings,
and she was certain her bones had been worn brittle,
stilts of a house helpless against a hurricane.

But this is the beauty of grief.

What she saw in the mirror was not
the deep ravine left by loss.
The war she was waging
had not hollowed her cheeks or made an anarchy
of her skin. Her lips had not unpinked from slaughter.

Instead, a pliancy and sheen had birthed from the rubble.
The eyes looking back at her were bright as promises
and it wasn't the overhead light or the sudden April sun.
Grief had lifted the rawness out of her,
clutched at the throat of her darkness and pulled
until it lay silent and sleeping at her feet,
a feral dog fed and full,
and what was left was neither muscle nor wound
but horizon line, a ripe nothingness,
some fresh story beginning,
etching her face clean.

the velocity of tulips

It happens like this. One evening you are buying cereal
and packaged mushrooms and accepting a paper cup sample
of the store's decaf French Roast. The aisles are crowded
as always. You've just come from the gym. Someone is hogging
the cheese display. You see them shifting their weight between
the triple crème and the fat-free. A mother is wrestling a cart
bearing gallons of organic milk and a squirrelly toddler.
The lines to the cashier remind you a little of those images
following a natural disaster, the filing behind a single water source,
just inches from mayhem. You fall in step like the little soldier you are,
plucking a bag of wheat bread from the tall, soft stack,
zeroing in on a package of free-range chicken thighs,
deciding against the bottle of wine and the sour-sweet jellybeans
and the frozen pizza that previously disappointed.
You remember you're about to run out of detergent
and you consider the cost of artichokes and put one back.
But then, tulips.

You see them out of the corner of your eye,
yellow cups firing out of a thick stalk of storybook green.
You'd avoided their gaze coming into the store, the signs
with bubble letters chirping their praises. Spring
is not yet here, but the tulips are,
hatched from some cozy hothouse stateside.
You are the kind of person who bypasses cherries
peddled prematurely in a market banking on your ignorance.
You do not visit the Rose Garden in December,
hopeful of a harvest. You are suspicious of the terminally
unripe avocados erupting like Vesuvius down the center aisle.
You stick to timelines, to patience, to the limits of the season.

But where has that gotten you?
When will you stop believing happiness will be retrieved
only after a blistering trial of error?

You are the instrument, the causeway,
the tunnel, the hand, the song
slicing through that air. You do not need a miracle to see that light.

Something is calling to you. Tulips, and whatever will come after.
It takes just 10 steps of your time to cross the store.
It takes a religious conversion of the most plebian proportions.
An empty vase rests on the top of your refrigerator, waiting.
This is no impotent vessel bridging you to freedom.
This is what will make beauty happen in your own kitchen,
when you come up the stairs after the day has spit you out,
when you have become lost in the woods of your own making.
This is what will greet you:
Yellow and stem and glass and the lifeblood of water.
You are certain of this now, with that clutch of ripe color
in your hands. You are certain this is the moment your heart will break
of its malnourishment and you will lift your fists out of the mud.
You are certain because the door slides open and your body
is already leaning into the breeze
as if it could carry the whole weight of you.
As if it already is.

sitting Shiva for Muriel Katz

The bowl of fruit on the dining room table
is brimming with kiwi. Outside it is snowing,
New England December in full throttle. She was not
a woman I've ever met. In fact, I've never been to this house
before this afternoon, when my mother and I came in
with a cake and an offer to help set up the chairs.
Jacqui was home from Rochester, grief
gripping her eyelids. She let me kiss her cheek
as my mother introduced us. I didn't know quite
what to say. My own grandfather had died the same day
Muriel went under for the last time. They were buried
on a Tuesday, an hour apart. I had been unable to come
to his funeral, and last night's delayed flight
kept me from sitting the final Shiva. Instead, I was holed up
in an airport hotel in Philadelphia, squeezing a tube of bath bubbles
into a tub too hot to get into.
I wish I could tell you it was Jacqui I came for,
or the memory of her mother, who'd collapsed from a stroke
and never returned. I wish I could tell you I gazed
at the photos set out in the living room as if I knew
what kind of loss this was, as if I could begin to shape
the life they illuminated. But when the service began
I found myself at the outskirts of the circle, on a folding chair set
next to the fruit salad, a stack of paper plates, coffee cake,
spinach quiche, a bowl of dried apricots, store-bought salsa, and kugel.
I said the prayers, rose when the rabbi asked, faced the proverbial ark
where the Torah scrolls would be, but when I turned to sit down again
it was my mother's face I saw, her hand cradling Jacqui's,
and I thought to myself, How did she get so strong?

Yet there was something of the survivor in her, too,
the faintest frailty, papery as my grandfather's wrists.
I felt it in her touch as I stepped off the plane,
twelve hours later than I was expected, the cradle
her hands gave my lower back, the bag she had packed
with a firm, tart apple, a container of yoghurt, the Danish
bought that morning from Henion's Bakery.
"In case you're hungry," she'd said, as I swung my legs
into the passenger seat and we pulled onto the highway heading north,
and there was a new softness to her voice, a porousness
I took for heartache but which, perhaps, was heartache's opposite –
the great yielding of love, blood unburdened at last.

Muriel was a woman with enviable eyebrows.
She looked good in a dress. I could imagine her late husband,
Morris, holding onto her arm on a steep flight of stairs.
There was something entirely solid about her.
I wondered if Jacqui had inherited her hands,
those thick fingers. I wondered if she had been handed down
the recipe for the chicken soup now warming in the Crockpot.
There was so much I didn't know.

My grandfather would have said something about the kiwi.
He would have remarked about the brightness of that green
against the strawberries, the sun-gold pineapple.
He would have taken a pinch of apricots from the bowl,
cut a generous slice of coffee cake, talked to the strangers
in the room about his daughter. "She was a dancer," he would have said,
before moving onto other things.

We stand for the Mourner's Kaddish and suddenly
they are both there, Muriel and my grandfather,

each flanking the daughter left among this living world,
and then quiche is served in uneven triangles,
and there is the accidental spill of a plastic cup of seltzer,
and the dog is running underfoot and there is someone
with allergies, and the kugel is cold and no one brought decaf,
and I don't want to die until I am goddamned good and ready,
and outside the snow keeps falling and falling and falling.

intermission

And so they will rise from their seats,
fan out into the hall, head straight
for the bar or the bathroom or
to call the babysitter and check on the kids.
And the stage will lose its currency, its showmanship,
the actors their roles. The story will throw its lines
into the fire. And this act of dispersal
will bring the lobby to life. A hum
will overtake the walls, the marble floor
warming with the to-ing and fro-ing of shoes.
Perfumes will collide and the hems of dresses will touch,
fleetingly, in the foyer of the ladies' room.
Lovers will mingle unknowingly with widows,
artists with politicians, children of assaultive alcoholics
with secret, sweet drunks. There will be a pinking of cheeks
from the unexpected heat, dollars absentmindedly pressed
into tip jars, and an innocent exchange under a balustrade
will produce a phone number and magical thinking.
Someone will almost slip on a square of dropped ice. Another
will drum up the plot of his next novel or realize that he must stop
writing altogether. Spouses will lean close for one clarification
or another, or try to remember the name of the couple just approaching.
A glimmer of hope will twist and spin from the small space
of held hands. Ghosts of a cottony memory will slide from the balcony:
five years old and the first matinee, 12 years and that unbearable opera,
19 in the aftermath of sex; 23 in the aftermath of their divorce.
The line will seem so long until it doesn't.
Lipstick will be reapplied, a matte pucker inked into a tissue.
A man will offer a handkerchief to someone unfamiliar.
Bodies will weave and sway like a school of fish around a carcass.

It will not last long.
Disorder is typically, almost predictably brief.
A bell will ring and a light will flicker and they will know
that this limbo between acts is coming to a close.
They will climb up the stairs to their little square seats
and decide, again, which of the arm rests is theirs and they will
tighten one thigh against the other to thwart an accidental touch
with a neighbor. Their gaze will ignore everything
but the stage and the curtains will draw back and the music will begin
and they will disappear into the shadows and be quiet about it
as the spotlight halos down below.
In the dark, their shoulders will hunch down.
The playbill will tighten in their fists,
and the story will rise from the ashes and reassemble,
and the actors will continue their charade.

Were it not for the untidy clatter on hard stone.
Were it not for the weight of shifting legs and the curving line.
Were it not for the fracturing of silence and memory.
Were it not for the unrehearsed.
Were it not for longing.
Were it not for error.
Were it not for uncertainty.
Were it not for collision and undoing and mess.
Were it not for thirst and risk and love,
the show
would never go on.

exit

Maybe it was wrong to have this conversation
in the parking lot of the highest point in the city,
the view spreading out below like caramel praline,
all that coastline, those hills, that water, those skyscrapers,
the air, pushing through this crack of mountain and radio tower
and rifling the tourists' hairdos and windbreakers
as they sat in silence on giraffe-print seat covers,
a white rose wilting between them.
Maybe the first of June was ill-timed as the day
to let go, admit defeat, cut the story
at its knees and offer the lackluster, conciliatory gesture
of a hug. Perhaps she shouldn't have worn the blouse
with the flattering neckline, or the necklace with the circle -
green and earthy - at its center, or the cowl-hooded coat
that could easily warm two bodies on such a blustery afternoon.
Maybe she should have waited until they were both home
in their separate apartments and made the announcement
by phone, so when the call ended the retreat would not have included
the loaded silence of the car, or the movie crew cordoning off
the lot below to set up the big shot, or the rescue helicopter
karate-chopping the sky, or the golden spokes of sun
that landed on the dashboard and cast cinematic shadows of their profiles.
Maybe it was wrong to want to end on this note with their bodies
awkwardly proximate, and the sand from their nap on the beach
two days ago still clinging to the caddy where the water bottle had been,
and the seagull feather that had whispered thoughts of flight
into her ear now resting comfortably in the center of the back seat.
Maybe it was wrong not to look directly in the eye and say
what needed saying, and instead have the words bubble out
into the steering column, then slant left to the change holder.

Love is never an exact science. The choreography goes
unrehearsed, its arms noodly as a teenage boy's.
An effort at grace is attempted then thwarted. The perfume
sours, the belly bloats, the syllables sputter and halt,
and she is struck by the incongruities between them now,
the way the news slices them in two, frays them
like spent wires. There is nothing left to do, and that,
perhaps, is the saddest thing, the room of them gutted to the bone,
and an emptiness whistling through.
But this is the only way. She knows this like she knows
the far corners of a basketball court, where the sweetest
shot lives. Like the heat of a tealight in the middle
of a power outage, how the palms could cup that warmth forever.
She knows this like the sound of alley cats and rain and home.
Like that place on the back of the neck that stays
tender and forgiving, ready to arch itself up and stretch its flesh
to meet the next great kiss.

placeholder

Say heater is another word for love
and the rug in the entryway, dusted with bits
of whatever I carried in at the bottom of my shoes
is another word for loyalty. Winter is another word
for patience, and of course kitchen is a combination
of two words - earth and body - and laundry basket
is another word for tired. Television is another word
for forget the story and art is another word
for tell it again. Window is another word for
acceptance and dinner is another word for us.
The track's bouncy pink surface is another word
for return to where you came from, and the calluses
from rock climbing are another word for hang on.
This moment is another word for where did the time go and
the doctor's bill is another word for luck. The bedside lamp
is another word for waiting. Silence is another way
of saying it. Tea is another word for mother.
Orgasm is another word for God.
Ambulance, for gratitude. Sweater, for not ready.
Book is another word for innocence.
Rain too, and mint chocolate chip, and slippers, and sleep.
You are another word for me, and I am another word for you.
Dream is another word for fear and hope, and so is loss.
Sunlight is another word for try again. The hail at the cemetery,
for believe in miracles. Buckle your seat belts for
don't leave just yet. Late March is another word for
you are where you are. Muscle is another word for yearning.
Mud puddle is another word for permission, and sink
is another word for letting go. Swallow is another word for
breathe, and breathe is another word for one more chance

and one more chance is another word for I will get this wrong again,
I can promise you.
So forgive me. This will all be imperfect.
No matter how I say it, it will never be the same as what it is.
But here. Take this beach pail and the shovel too. These
are other words for come with me, for keep digging,
for we're almost there.

the recital

The billboard on the highway said it would be
Judgment Day, so I suppose I should have thought twice
about taking the subway, lest the power fail
and humanity begin its terrible unraveling underground.
But not a hitch delayed the departure
or arrival of the J Church, and I rise out of the
Van Ness steps buffeted by the strong bay wind.
Two miles away, a baseball game
is in its first optimistic innings, but here the streets
are almost deserted, the parking lot of the Conservatory
a skeleton of its weekday twin.
If this turns out to be my last evening on earth,
I muse, at least there will be music.
And soon, a young man takes the stage, suit-
and-tied 17-year-old, and begins, by heart,
Beethoven's Sonata in C minor. I wish my father
was sitting next to me – I can already imagine the
glee in his face, the way his fingers would begin
their pantomime on his lap, remembering. At intermission,
we would reminisce about the duets we played,
and there would be a moment I'd admit regretting stopping altogether,
watching this boy-man coax stories out of the keys, and wonder
if perhaps I took a wrong turn somewhere, or left prematurely,
fearing the discipline or disappointment, whichever came first.
And then I would remember, no, this is exactly where I needed to be,
listening, listening, leaning back into my squeaky seat and simply
paying attention.

The concert continues, unapocalyptic. The building doesn't fall.
Night slides by like it always does, one hour then another.

There is still time enough for everything,
and I know this because when the boy-man takes his bow
it's clear the story hasn't ended, all that is yet to be written
and played, waiting waiting waiting. On the tip of his fingers,
at the doorway, on the stairs, in the empty parking lot,
on the rustling tracks and on early summer bleachers,
under this dark and possible sky.

how we are not alone

Because a light on the other side of the street reveals
someone more insomniac than you.
Because the camera made its way into the carry-on,
not for the traveler, but those staying behind.
Because the daisy, its boastful yellow,
begged for a closer look.
Because you found yourself being stared at
by horses.
Because the church bell rang precisely at noon,
and all of the stores slid closed.
Because someone else's charcoal fire
made your own mouth water.
Because you are afraid of losing him
in a crowd.
Because of the mournful sound of train whistles.
Because your father let you see him cry.
Because a palm against a cheek
steers the world into softer focus.
Because the poplars insist on
weathering the winter.
Because of lighthouses.
Because of shadows.
Because of a shared memory of perfume.
Because of the sound of feet on cobblestones.
Because of window boxes.
Because of the man spinning pizza dough
like a circus act.
Because the apple tree freed itself of dessert.
Because you could hear the waterfall
from a mile away.

Because she understands
your every look.
Because the martini glasses came in fours.
Because the cashier's hand grazed yours,
despite the coins between you.
Because even if the first words fail,
the next ones won't.
Because the car in the next lane signaled left.
Because of the stone wall you found in the woods.
Because the dog returns at a single whistle.
Because of the brilliant descent of leaves,
and the pile that beckoned the neighbors.
Because a handful of blackberries saved you
the last miles home.
Because there are nights the stars look
as if they're winking.

begin here

When the last seat is taken,
or the key has trapped in the lock.
When the rain has eviscerated your garden,
or your words have run out one by one.
When the packing is half-finished, or traffic
keeps you from your purpose.
When the bright white of your day
has paled and pixilated.
When the grocery bag rips coming up the stairs.
When the telephone bill shocks
and then flounders you.
When love has flown off course.
When your nails are ragged and wanton.
When the runway is slick and the sky sodden.
When the ache for something nameless
fans out into your bones.
When you're hungry, or lost or in need of a hand
across your eyelashes.
When it's deadline or dilemma
or just you tripping on the stained carpet of your trouble,
begin here.

Place one leaden, obstinate foot
where you can see it.
Gather your maniacal breath,
your little windbags of lungs.
Eye only the square of sidewalk a blink away,
that quadrant of concrete mottled with the dirty
evidence of living,
and go.

When the manual for what's broken
has been misplaced. When the view is obscured
by a restless construction site.
When your closet is an echo of castoffs.
When the bridge toll climbs and the road
down the mountain is pummeled with snow.
When your face bears little resemblance
to the person you remember.
When the field is populated with abler bodies.
When poems have been written by nimbler souls.
When no amount of squinting
delivers oasis, begin here.

Guide your defeated arms
into a small fit of swinging.
Coerce your hips into the barest
shimmy. Locate the pocket of a single,
deserted minute, its hum of insignificance,
and go.

When cheer cannot cheer you,
when crumbs cannot feed you,
when the storage space in the garage
topples from the weight.
When beauty eludes you.
When the weatherman confirms your fear.
When the doctor bears his wild news.
When you return to the bad habit.
When the current continues its brutal tackle.
When mess is your middle name,
begin here.

Climb onto your weary haunches. Lift your belly
from its mattress cave. Initiate the wholly
unremarkable act of breathing, and go.

When you have had enough.
When you have had too much.
When your fortress has not kept away the enemy,
and the walls are an abscess of rubble.
Do not fling yourself from the gangplank.
Do not hasten your disappearance
with your own cruelty.
Do not mask your ferocity with a collage of good manners.

The death's door of your failure
is still a door.
Wrap your shaking fist around the handle.
Hear the cricket click of the latch.
And begin.

what happiness was

I wish I could picture the whole of 176 South Bath Avenue for the two years our family lived there, just a short drive away from the Blue Ridge Mountains. I was seven when we moved there, nine when we left, and though I could tell you about the living room with my grandmother's hand-me-down television that spun out Saturday morning cartoon, that's not what sticks. There was that backyard where my sister and I set a tent up once for an overnight sleepover with Bea and Janet from down the street, and where Janet threw up after too much pizza, and there was the playroom upstairs that I had to give up when my brother was born. I could tell you something about the time I stole into the kitchen while my parents were having choir rehearsal and licked off all the chocolate frosting off a cake my father had made for after, and the spanking I got for that. Or the glass cabinet my sister rocked the rocking chair into while we were playing Scrabble, her scalp sliced open and the river of blood running down her forehead, and how I screamed louder than she did, the pain etched in my own body just watching her.

But it's the house across the street I remember most vividly, where Zach and Shawn lived, and the afternoons I'd spend there after school, playing basketball in their side yard, the leather of the ball still palpable in my hands, the stark whiteness of my skin against theirs, and this strange new feeling of symmetry as we shuffled down the half-court defending each other, throwing wild shots into the air, laughing. I had been such a creature of solitude, content to entertain myself with the smallest thing, hunkered down on my knees for hours watching ants and making swirls in the dirt, dreaming of God knows what. I had thought this the greatest pleasure. But no. The conversation between bodies at play. Contact pure and simple. I don't think I knew what happiness was, until this.

to love what we love

In the retelling, we'll say we surrendered. We'll say it was fate.
There is the sweet narrative we'll draft from the complicated geography
that somehow pulled our continents together. We'll chart the tides,
the turning leaves, the particular intelligences responsible for how the story
found its edge, that pivotal moment of knowing.

But first, what must birth out of us is trouble,
heart-legs buckling under, the muscle shoring us to solitude
sliced limp. The devastation will not be minor.
We will cut and claw ourselves away from the sharp, new light.
We will brutalize ourselves with escape.

But out of this flight and anguish a vacancy will appear,
hollowness we will mistake, initially, as loss. Here, here is where
the real beginning begins, swiping us naked from our hiding place,
imprinting our skin. We will be astonished
we are even alive. The cold air will feel like the slimmest kind of luck.

And then, this: A space will warm and soften around us.
We will gather the silence in at the corners.
We will squint at this unfamiliar shape of peace.
And from here, fresh breathing room for love, our bodies leaning
close and steady, the hum of a radiator underneath the floorboards,
our mouths petal-wet, opening to the first, honest kiss.

We won't be able to stop it. Coming alive is impossible to fix
into a single embrace. The dismantling will pull the river out of us,
and we will fall against the other in a wellspring of raw relief.
The language will be a stranger on our tongues but
we will understand it perfectly: to love what we love

is an undoing, a deliberate fall with our palms out,
hunger with the grief torn out of it. If it is surrender,
it is to the confession that we are worthy. If it is fate,
it is to the irrepressible freedom that bubbles from our darkest places.

There is no going back, our gaze wrenched away
from a lock-jawed past, the bones of us already fusing,
the sky wide above in the perfect V of flocking geese,
and a clear and faithful morning
welcoming us awake.

yes

yes
yes
after a violent rain
bloody battle on the roof
mud-inked, wind-broken
roots chunked and hazardous
the velocity of the river a cause
for posted signs and nervous dogs
yes
yes
to blisters on shoulders from too much
sun, mouth woolly, limbs limp
as old dandelions yes
to skinned knees and black-bruised
egos, shyness and tongue-tripping yes
yes yes to the slow crawl of indecision
to remorse to hideous mistake
to saccharine and over-salted
to no vacancy and lost chances
yes to the ugly failures in front
of the hometown crowd
to oversized and under-whelmed
to cheats and lies and cowards
yes to the rips in your new silk dress
to torn up and torn down
yes to the conversation
you didn't want to have
to irrational, irreconcilable, irreversible words
yes to cracked throats and busted ankles and spent light bulbs
and burned batteries and whatever dies after

it has lived
yes
to a broken promise or three or nine hundred
yes to the time it takes to tell the truth
yes to desert and dry spells and lunacy and lost hope
yes to the middle of a blind-white October
yes yes yes
to sharp and scrape and cauterize
to discard and done for
yes to ducking under yes to darkness
to breaking in two
or more pieces
than you can count
yes to the disappointing lunch
to the disappointing summer
to the disappointing marriage
yes to the seesaw fear of stillness and escape
yes to the bad haircut in eighth grade that ruined your chances
yes to the fumbling in the back seat that led
to your bad reputation
yes to beyond repair
to what's done is done
to a change of heart mid-stream
yes to bad art
to old age
to out of shape and shapeless
yes to where have you been
and why didn't you call
and how many times do I have to tell you
yes all of it yes
not a moment too soon or too late
this yes, this yes

this ripe and mad and fleshy terror of a thing
this yes will save us
tie our restless shoelaces and stroke
our fevered cheeks and pay off our
inglorious debts
this yes, this yes
this aching starved animal
will bear down until we open ourselves
to its wet mouth and slip our skin
under its teeth and feel its dark heart beating
ruthless against our lungs and let our heaviness fall
like a string of dominoes until we sing
our fragile, damaged beauty
into the waiting arms of the world.

the window seat

This might have been it, the window seat, 14A, on the Delta flight to Atlanta with the man in 14B with the ruined left thumbnail and the woman beside him deep in the heart of romance novel. This might have been it, Palm Sunday and April Fool's, the cloud layer out of Hartford and the sky a perfectly perfect blue and the flight attendant with the whitest teeth you've ever seen. Or this could have been it, the mashed-up front of your Toyota Echo on the back roads of Western Massachusetts in the middle of an eerily early snowstorm, with your friend beside you with the aunt who died on this same day 15 years ago thousands of feet over Nova Scotia. Or this: a tumor the size of an Easter egg hugging the top quadrant of your spinal cord, and the slow diminishment of your body before the surgeons took over. This might have been it, the Rogue River in Oregon when you were 25 and catapulted underneath and inside the great rapids in your tiny, inflatable kayak. Or this, like poor Reggie Lewis with the Boston Celtics, his young heart failing in the middle of practice some spring afternoon. Or this, just now: the labyrinth and the trio of horses and the tree that may or may not be a dogwood, and Southern birds singing their late afternoon song, and the white mug of strong coffee Celeste made to your right, and the sound of the wicker chair as you write in your near illegible cursive on this first Monday in April. All of it, interrupted by an unforeseen meteor or brain stem stroke like the one Deb's brother had which took away everything except his memory of math. This might have been it, the awkward confrontation with your mother, the long silence with your brother, the fall at the Embarcadero ice rink, the first time you knew you were making love with someone else, the panna cotta you made from scratch with whole vanilla bean, your kitchen morphing into Madagascar, the sunburn from that black sand beach in Barbados, the crossword puzzle you fought your sister for, the lightning storm on Skinner Mountain, the algebra test you barely passed, the knowing that swept you like a flood out the door with a single suitcase and a one-way ticket. This might have been it, but it wasn't. It wasn't. You weren't. You squirreled into a small patch of sun. You blinked a sliver of light into the rooms of your dark house. You found the fingers of a hand that came out of nowhere to look for yours. You rose from your knees and lived.

toward summit

You bring a pad of paper, of course, and the good
pen because you imagine the hike will ask for your keenest
observation, and this you take to mean words
you will lay down on that even white acreage. And so you climb
in earnest without a water bottle like some fool thing,
toward summit, pushing your knees through the bush
and eyeing the blond earth forming the semblance of a path.
Even from here, you can imagine yourself at the higher elevation,
the scansion that view will allow, and the lines that will
river out of you, an ode you will craft out of this mountain,
and how you might – you dare say – turn it even more beautiful,
mythic with beauty. At the first quarter-mile, in fact,
you're already clicking the metaphors off your tongue,
dreaming up better ways to say "green" and "wide" and "wild."
The rock where you're heading becomes a man,
a lover, God, beckoning you close, and soon
your fingers are itchy to transcribe the conversation.
There is a poem in your mouth, its scrawny beginnings,
and you push it down against your chest with every step and
breath by breath to make it flesh.

But if you were really here, you would know
you're not looking where you should. For instance,
there are a thousand ways to break
your leg, and there are the bees to consider,
the flicker of rattlesnake, the ground sand-dry
and near avalanche at the steepest inclines.
There is the nature of this nature.
Three quarters of the way up a thirst encroaches
on your throat. It has become so hot outside,

breezeless, the brush leaving thistly markings on your ankles.
The paper moistens and droops in your sweaty hand,
the pen slips to the ground, and so do you,
landing on the plateau from which the summit
flirts and cajoles. In front of you,
a trail of ants soldiers back and forth,
carrying invisible rations.
You don't know about ants, if these are the ones
that will level with you with one bite
or simply industrious vegetarians. No matter.
They are ignoring you. You could sit here as long as you like,
eavesdropping. Various birds are circling – you don't know
their names, but you know, at least, they are birds.
Maybe that is all that's required, to recognize
what you're looking at, because your mind is a trickle, now,
slow as summer noon. The poem slips out, unseen,
from your teeth. The word for wild is "wild,"
and the trees below are continent enough.
There can be no more green to this green.
If you could just sit here,
watching them move as they move,
still as they still, breathing your wordless breaths
until your lungs understand, you will have it.
This is the poem.
This.

witness

I wish you could see this, me hovering over a breakfast
I woke early to make, ripe mangoes and coins
of sliced banana, blueberries, the smell of shallots
sautéed in olive oil, and the eggs waiting for the guests
to arrive to be gentled into the pan, then scrambled.
I wish you could have been here for the small catastrophe
I made of the scones, confusing baking soda for powder,
but how beautiful they were, despite their bitterness.
If you had been here, I would have given you a turn
with the crepe batter, guided your wrists through the swirl
of the pan, cautioned you against waiting too long and
we would have clinked coffee cups, toasting our good fortune
or the still heat of this place, flies catatonic on the deck,
or the way summer uncoils us, softens our grip, makes a smooth
line of our previous disrepair. I would have liked to show you
the fledgling grape vines, driven you to the market and stood agape
at the price of strawberries, wondered aloud if the trail
through the woods led to a waterfall, and turned off the final light
to listen to the concert of crickets. I wish you could be here
as the day unlatches and spreads open, and see the wide green
of the back field as the man on the small tractor makes his
perfect tracks, and sit under these motionless trees, and swat
the occasional mosquito, and read our books until the heat
lays us flat.

I have to remember that solitude doesn't make the story
less true. The sun births the same sweat from the inside
of my elbows, and the cream has turned my coffee
just as caramel. I am still in love with the thinness
and roundness of crepes and the way they hold

so much more than their own weight.
If I can hold my hands through the quiet.
If I can bless the air with my own breathing.
If I can imagine the possibility of waterfall.
If I can bite into the flesh of this mango
and still know sweetness,
perhaps that is witness enough.

unpublished work

The hibiscus needs a poem,
the grasshopper too – he looked so unbearably vulnerable
in the middle of that island road.
Low tide deserves a poem about
the importance of retreat, and the woman
who rang up the groceries was carrying a poem
about loss, eyebrows pinching when she gave me the receipt.
The two boys at the playground, see-sawing themselves into a fight,
need a poem in which war is given a long set of parables
from childhood. Breakfast is ripe with poetry, the tangle of mango
and omelet and limbs of sausage and the exclamation point
the raspberry jam makes against the tongue.
Laurie needs a poem, the sweat on her obliques
midway through the workout video, the primitive grunt
at the home stretch, and how peaceful she looks
with that second cup of coffee.
The flight over the Pacific is brimming with metaphor,
the incongruities of small window and vast sky and the glass
barring one from the other. Eli's laughter is begging
for a poem, the universe of hope it carries with it
and how the tuck of his hand crossing a busy street
delivers an almost excruciating joy. Rain
is ruthless with poetry, that great cleansing of history.
The canyon trail could use a verse or two,
its wildness gentrified by the cellophane wraps
of cigarette packs and tennis balls abandoned
in thickets by dogs weary of the search.
The piano needs a poem, that Mozart duet
unplayed for three decades still poised
somewhere at the edge of the edge of fingertips.

The golf course wouldn't think to ask
but it needs a poem, too, its green hips flirting
with a ceaseless manicure, the strange marriage
it makes of fact and fiction. The highway
craves a poem, Route 2 carving an additional solitude
from northern Montana, the wearying stretch of the Panhandle,
towns on the brink of disappearance, and dust
heavy on the windshield. A poem lies in this living room,
vacation magazines and sunscreen sharing real estate
with a notebook and a pen that may run out at any moment.
And so the poet, too, needs a poem, to remind herself
of the unpublished work, life waking to its first pulse,
body rising toward inklings of light,
the heart stirring itself open, already knowing
it will break.

Maya Stein is a poet, writing facilitator and creative adventurer. She has published two collections of personal essays, "The Overture of an Apple" and "Spinning the Bottle," as well as "Enough Water," a collection of poetry and photographs, and has kept a weekly 10-line poetry practice ("10-line Tuesday") since 2005. In 2010, Maya completed "Tour de Word," a two-month, 30-state traveling poetry project that brought no-cost writing workshops to more than 200 people. This past summer, she embarked on a second traveling project, "Type Rider," a 40-day, 1,300-mile bicycling and typewriting journey from Amherst, MA to Milwaukee, WI. Maya dabbles in hair cutting, ran a small catering business for six years, took part in a Ringling Bros' and Barnum & Bailey Circus act for one afternoon, and has been writing poetry since she was nine. Learn about these adventures and more at www.mayastein.com